Srimad
Bhagavad Gita
– Essence

Commentary on selected 90 verses (Slokas)

Srimad Bhagavad Gita
— Essence

Commentary on selected 90 verses (Slokas)

By
Dr N K Srinivasan

V&S PUBLISHERS

Published by:

V&S PUBLISHERS

F-2/16, Ansari road, Daryaganj, New Delhi-110002
☎ 23240026, 23240027 • *Fax:* 011-23240028
Email: info@vspublishers.com • *Website:* www.vspublishers.com

Regional Office : Hyderabad
5-1-707/1, Brij Bhawan (Beside Central Bank of India Lane)
Bank Street, Koti, Hyderabad - 500 095
☎ 040-24737290
E-mail: vspublishershyd@gmail.com

Branch Office : Mumbai
Jaywant Industrial Estate, 2nd Floor–222, Tardeo Road
Opposite Sobo Central Mall, Mumbai – 400 034
☎ 022-23510736
E-mail: vspublishersmum@gmail.com

Follow us on:

All books available at **www.vspublishers.com**

© **Copyright: V&S Publishers**
ISBN 978-93-813849-1-6
Edition 2015

The Copyright of this book, as well as all matter contained herein (including illustrations) rests with the Publishers. No person shall copy the name of the book, its title design, matter and illustrations in any form and in any language, totally or partially or in any distorted form. Anybody doing so shall face legal action and will be responsible for damages.

Printed at : Param Offseters, Okhla, New Delhi-110020

Dedication
This book is dedicated to
MY LORD
Shirdi Sainath

Contents

Preface	09
Introduction	15
1. JNANA YOGA	29
2. KARMA YOGA	39
3. BHAKTI YOGA	43
4. DHYANA YOGA	52
5. YOGA OF RENUNCIATION	56
6. SYNTHESIS OF YOGAS AND THE PATH OF SURRENDER	60
7. THE COSMIC FORM	68
Bibliography	71

Preface

The Bhagavad Gita, also known as 'The Lord's Song' or 'The Song Celestial', is a Hindu scripture that represents the essence of Vedanta for millions of Hindus. Because of the universality of its message, it goes far beyond being merely a Hindu text. In truth, it is a formula for successful living, valid for all time—an imperishable spiritual heritage bequeathed to all humanity.

This long poem is of 700 verses, in fairly straightforward Sanskrit. Several English translations are available. It is, however, a formidable task to study and to assimilate the essence of this long scripture. Therefore a shorter version – a condensation with only about 90 verses – is attempted in this book. This should appeal to modern readers who have limited time or are less inclined to study the full text.

The Gita is divided into 18 chapters; each chapter has been labelled a yoga or Upanishad. This apparently convenient division, however, suffers from a severe limitation in that certain concepts are repeated and re-introduced in several chapters. Traditional teachers and preachers discuss the chapters one by one either by way of written texts or in the form of discourses, from Chapter 1 to Chapter 18. Some scholars choose to focus on only one or two chapters in their discourses. I have adopted a different approach; the verses are presented thematically. For instance, in Jnana yoga, all relevant verses from Chapters 1 to 18 are presented in sequence.

I have selected and explained Jnana yoga, Karma yoga, Bhakti yoga, Dhyana yoga and Sannyasa yoga in separate chapters. Another chapter – Synthesis of yogas – presents other verses that are a kind of summary and the ultimate message of 'surrender'. A final chapter briefly narrates the 'Cosmic Form' displayed by the Lord to Arjun—a condensation of Chapter 11 of the Gita. I hope this thematic condensation would be easy to follow and make the concepts and messages clearer to readers.

I have provided brief annotations/notes after most of the verses. These notes clarify certain terms, explain specific points, or touch upon any conflicting views relating to a particular verse. A few notes provide historical perspective in relation to Vedic times, the practices that were then prevalent, and the later trends.

As a Vedantic text, the Gita is a superb summary of the Upanishads. Traditional scholars include three texts of Vedanta–Upanishads, Brahma Sutras and the Gita – as a trilogy: foundational texts (prasthaana triya). 'Lord Krishna is the divine milkman, the Upanishads are the cows, and the Gita is the milk obtained for the sake of Arjun and all mankind', states a poem.

The Upanishads and the Brahma Sutras are admittedly difficult texts to study. The Gita is much simpler and delightful to read and follow. It is of later origin than the Upanishads, but perhaps precedes the Brahma Sutras. Therefore, it can be inferred that the Gita is an improved version of Upanishadic teachings. The Bhakti or devotional aspects are merely mentioned in the Upanishads, while Bhakti yoga (devotional path) occupies a major part of the Gita. As such, the Gita is much more than a mere summary of the Upanishads.

I have mentioned that the Gita is delightful to read and easy to follow. One of the reasons for this is that it takes the form of a dialogue between Arjun and the Lord, Sri Krishna. While dialogues exist in the Upanishads too, they are heavy and use abstruse terms. Arjun raises many everyday questions that trouble a person's mind. The Lord's answers to these dilemmas of day-to-day existence are direct and specific, hence the powerful appeal of this text to scholars and lay persons alike.

Many scholars have interpreted the Gita as essentially a document emphasising Karma yoga (selfless action) or Jnana yoga (the path of knowledge or enquiry), or even the path of devotion and surrender (Bhakti yoga). The Gita is much more than this. It is a superb integration of several yogas, for it is hardly possible to practice any one yoga in isolation. It is this synthesis that is unique in the Gita. Unfortunately, this point has been overlooked by many translators who are content with literal interpretations, preferring to rely on word-for-word translations, or by appending specific notes based on sectarian beliefs with a slant towards one of the yogas. The present book gives the integrated view of yogas as elucidated by the Lord.

There are more than 250 commentaries on the Gita. The main commentaries have come from the three great Acharyas—Adi Sankara, Sri Ramanuja and Sri Madhwa. Many others have followed these, with minor variations. However, these are sectarian-based commentaries. Which commentary should one follow?—I have preferred not to follow any one commentary, but have taken specific views and interpretations for each verse, guided largely by my own intuitive perception—what seemed most suitable for a given verse. While doing so, I have kept historical perspectives intact, because the commentaries are inevitably coloured by historical compulsions.

One should note that Sankara's commentary came about in the 9th century—almost three thousand years after the Mahabharata war and the original version of the Gita. (If the Gita was written sometime between the 3rd century BC and the 2nd century AD, then Sankara's work was written about a thousand years after the original manuscript was produced.) The passage of ten centuries would certainly have effected substantial changes in the social fabric, which would have inevitably impacted a commentator's interpretations and reflected his perceptions as coloured by the milieu prevalent at that time in history.

There is again a gap of nearly two hundred years between Sankara and Sri Ramanuja, and another gap of about a hundred years between Sri Ramanuja and Sri Madhwa. Therefore, one should not be surprised at the striking variations in their respective interpretations and sectarian beliefs. It is unfortunate, though, that sectarian beliefs have been allowed to undermine the force of the essential message given by the Lord. The modern reader can steer clear of these sectarian interpretations only by dint of considerable effort. This small book should be helpful in this respect.

I realise that selecting about 90 verses out of 700 is a highly subjective action. Another author might well have decided on a different assortment. However, I feel I have included all the important verses – the ones that are always heavily commented upon – as well as several others basically for the sake of maintaining coherency of presentation.

A detailed bibliography includes several works that are readily available to any English language reader. Some of the books mentioned therein address the subtle differences in interpretation and take the process to deeper levels appropriate for serious readers.

Above all, I hope that this small book will motivate the reader to study the full text with passion and devotion, and pursue spiritual goals towards liberation/moksha/nirvana/ eternal bliss or – in the Hindu context – freedom from the cycle of births and deaths or samsara.

Sarvam Krishnarapamastu !

—**Dr N K Srinivasan**

Introduction

The Bhagavad Gita is a Hindu scripture written in the Sanskrit language. It is presented in the form of a dialogue between Lord Krishna – the Supreme Being incarnated in human form, an avatar of Lord Vishnu – and the warrior-prince Arjun. It is set in the battlefield of Kurukshetra at the very outset of the Mahabharata war. As we all know, the *Mahabharata* is one of the two great epics of the Hindus, the other being the *Ramayana*. As such, the Gita is an intrinsic part of the Mahabharata.

Lord Krishna assumes the role of Arjun's charioteer, and is also his friend, philosopher and guide. Arjun, along with his four Pandava brothers, had to fight this war against their cousins (the Kauravas) to regain their usurped lands and titles. The righteous war was forced on them, even though the five Pandavas settled for just five villages instead of half the kingdom that was their rightful share. The Kauravas refused to part with even five villages: thus precipitating internecine war between the two rival camps.

When Lord Krishna positions the horse-drawn chariot at a point midway between the two armies arrayed on either side, right in the middle of the battlefield, Arjun becomes despondent; he does not wish to lead the battle as the commander. He sees his own kinsmen among the ranks of the enemy, his spirit quails and the resolve to fight goes out of him. He sees his own teachers and preceptors, his acharyas, including Dronacharya, the maestro who taught him archery, in the opposite camp. He knows that he would be forced to kill many of them in the ensuing battle. His heart is greatly troubled. There is a storm of doubts in his mind about the apparent conflict between duty and ethics. How can he kill those venerable teachers? In anguish, Arjun throws down his great bow, Gandeeva, and laments to Krishna, "I cannot fight. I will renounce this world. I don't need this property."

Lord Krishna explains the situation in simple, direct terms: "This is a righteous war. You have to destroy the wrong doers. You are a warrior. You cannot run away from your duty. As a warrior, it is your duty to fight such a war. It does not ultimately matter *who* gets killed, for all die...and yet the essence of all is immortal and imperishable. It is all a divine maya."

The scripture is written in such a way that the confusion in Arjun's mind is laid bare. He wants to know why he should fight, what exactly his duty is, what happens when someone dies and so on. The battlefield situation serves as the ideal backdrop for the Lord to share the spiritual knowledge according to Hindu philosophy—in terms of soul or Atman and the Imperishable Being or Brahman who pervades the Universe. Sublime knowledge is thus imparted to humanity through the Lord's dialogue with Arjun.

The Bhagavad Gita contains 700 verses and is divided into 18 chapters. Each chapter is given a title as 'Yoga of ——'. Yoga means 'path'. Yoga also means union (with the Supreme). Thus, the word 'yoga' denotes both the method and the goal.

Many scholars would divide the whole book into three sections of 6 chapters each. The first six chapters expound on Jnana (knowledge) and Karma (action) yogas. The middle six chapters explain the Universe, its creation and the Supreme Being. The last six chapters explain the path of devotion or Bhakti yoga and the path of renunciation. While such division is very convenient as far as teaching is concerned, the various yogas are often mixed up in several chapters. Therefore, clear-cut separation into three sections is not really a viable solution.

Many scholars focus on specific chapters, such as Chapter 3 for Karma yoga, Chapter 12 for Bhakti yoga and so on. This process is perfectly acceptable if one's intention is to understand the basic concepts. In fact, a beginner should first focus on only a few chapters, say Chapters 2, 3, 5, 9, 12 and 18 to gain some insight into the whole text. If someone confines his study only to Chapter 3, Chapter 9 and Chapter 12, for instance, he can still make substantial spiritual progress. Such is the power of the Gita. Many preachers just expound on one or two chapters in 5 to 10 hours of discourse.

For a serious reader, however, the study of all the 700 verses is a formidable undertaking. Therefore in this small book, we focus on only 90 verses—about one seventh of the original set. This subset would convey the complete message that has inspired generations of students of the Gita.

It is common practice to explain and paraphrase each chapter from Chapter 1 to Chapter 18. In such a method, several overlaps occur and some verses may even appear to contradict others.

In this book, we discuss different yogas in separate chapters and string together the corresponding verses from the Gita. This obviates repetition of ideas while retaining the systematic progression (and depth) of ideas as given in the original. One separate chapter titled 'Synthesis of yogas' provides verses that explain different yogas together.

The chapters are as follows:
- Jnana yoga (knowledge)
- Karma yoga (action)
- Dhyana yoga (meditation or raja yoga)
- Bhakti yoga (devotion)
- Sannyasa yoga (renunciation)
- Synthesis of yogas.

The last chapter summarises Chapter 11—the 'vishva roop darshan', where the Lord gives Arjun the divine power to see His Cosmic Form—the beatific vision showing the Glory of God.

The Yogas

The Gita is essentially a scripture explaining the different yogas or paths leading to spiritual liberation—Moksha or freedom from future births. This overriding spiritual goal is also stated in the Upanishads, as the goal of merging with the Brahman or the Supreme Being.

Lord Krishna takes pains to explain each type of yoga and also presents the integrated view of yogas. The Lord answers several specific questions raised by Arjun. Some are opening remarks or lead questions to get the dialogue started. Some questions relate to seeking clarifications or eliciting specific meanings from the Lord. Some questions are meant to fill the gaps in knowledge regarding soul, the world and the Supreme Being; they are mainly questions on Vedanta.

At one level of understanding, the Gita is essentially a

summary of the Upanishads. It is said that Lord Krishna is the divine milkman, milking the cow of the Upanishads to yield milk for Arjun and thereby for humanity at large. Several verses, in fact, are taken directly from the Upanishads, as we shall see later.

The Gita is one of the three foundational texts or scriptures, (prasthaana triya) the other two being the Upanishads and the Brahma Sutras. (While Upanishads are considered to pre-date the Gita chronologically, the Brahma Sutras are later texts).

Bhakti Yoga

Bhakti yoga or the path of Devotion is repeatedly stressed in the Gita. Earlier, the ritual part of the Vedas emphasised rituals and offerings to propitiate various Vedic gods, mostly for temporal benefits. Taking the lead from the Upanishads or the later part of the Vedas, the Gita emphasises the supreme importance of devotion to a Supreme Being or Brahman.

In fact, the Gita goes one step further. It calls for devotion to a Personal God, God in human form, in this case Lord Krishna Himself. What about those worshipping other gods? The Lord says in clear terms that if men worship other, lesser gods, their worship nevertheless still reaches Him alone. Therefore, it does not matter which God you worship as long as your heart (motive) is pure. The Lord repeatedly talks about single-minded devotion to Him.

Again, He rejects the elaborate rituals and sacrifices of Vedic times. One can worship the Lord with the simplest of means: a flower, a fruit, a leaf and even a few drops of water. Such is the stirring message of the Gita.

The Lord takes us to yet another – and higher –

stage. The easy path is to surrender to the Lord. The Lord protects your assets and rights in this world. He will remove all your sins, shower His grace on you and give you liberation and freedom from future births: the endless cycle of births and deaths we call Samsara. The Lord will give inner peace and bliss (ananda). He will also give you knowledge of Brahman. In short, you will realise sat-chit-ananda (existence-consciousness-bliss).

Karma Yoga

The Bhagavad Gita has another important message—the message of Karma yoga or Selfless Action. This is an amazingly original lesson from the Lord. In simple terms, it means: "Do your duty; do not crave for results; accept success and failure with equal calmness—unperturbed. You only have the right to do your duty—you have no claim on the results. Be detached from results, for they may bring name and fame one moment, and disgrace and ignominy the next. The man of wisdom remains unmoved in prosperity as well as in adversity, unmindful of whether he is criticised or glorified.

This message is of great significance for two reasons: Firstly, the Vedic literature extolled rituals and sacrifices that were mostly performed for personal gains: for prosperity, for progeny and for long stay in the heavenly abode. The Lord deprecates this in no uncertain terms. He says; "Do your duty and offer the fruits to the Lord. That is the highest form of sacrifice you can make". This message represents a radical departure from the ritualistic overtones of Vedic cults.

The second reason for the significance of this message is for Arjun and indirectly for all of us. Arjun was a warrior-prince inclined to shirk his duty of fighting a righteous war. The Lord tells Arjun that he should fight, doing his duty to the society even though he might have to kill his kinsmen and teachers. How often we are faced with similar dilemmas in our social and professional life? Should we do our duty boldly or run away from our responsibilities? The answer is clear: do your duty but leave the results to God.

In other words, we should surrender the results of our endeavours to God in the spirit of sacrifice. After all, it is God or Purusha who has given us this body, this life force or prana and this mind and intellect. We may understand how our body parts function and try to fix their problems—that is what medicine tries to do. But science has not been able to improve the design of any body part, nor has it managed to replicate any part perfectly without using stem cell technology, which is nothing but a way of recycling the original. We have grown from a single cell or fertilised egg into the complex organisms we are today. This contemplation should induce humility. When we surrender the outcomes of our actions to the Lord who has given us this body-mind-intellect to begin with, how can we be concerned about the results? We are then in His hands. Where is the need for fear?

According to Mahatma Gandhi, this message of Karma yoga is the central message of the Gita. He brought this out clearly in his lectures on the Gita delivered at Sabarmati Ashram, Ahmedabad in the 1920s.

There is, however, another philosophical standpoint: that Karma yoga and Bhakti yoga are preparatory steps for spiritual realisation and these only help us to purify our minds (chitta shuddhi). They may lead one to becoming a Jnana yogi. That is, liberation is possible only through Jnana yoga. This view was the main credo of Adi Sankara, the great Advaitic philosopher (788 – 820 AD) and his Advaitic school.

This view was disputed by later philosophers and saints who extolled bhakti (devotion) as the principal method, particularly Sri Ramanuja and others including Sant Kabir, Chaitanya Mahaprabhu and Sri Ramakrishna Paramahansa. Bhakti alone is sufficient for liberation.

Incidentally, this controversy led to much schism in the Hindu religion and led to the creation of several mutually antagonistic sects that were active till as late as the latter half of the 20th century. Such controversies also led to young people developing a strong distaste for sectarian traditions (sampradaya).

The view that Karma yoga is a valid path for self-realisation and that it is sufficient unto itself, is mainly due to Swami Vivekananda, the chief disciple of Sri Ramakrishna. This aspect will be examined further while discussing specific verses of the Gita.

This message of Karma yoga has great relevance for us today. We find many shirking their duties and responsibilities because they are apprehensive about the outcomes, i.e., results. Equanimity – taking success and failure, fame and disgrace as equal – is an attitude that is very difficult to cultivate, but cultivate it we must. The Lord says that equanimity (samatvam) is called Yoga.

We may not ever have to face great battles, as did Arjun, in our daily lives. But we do find ourselves locked in small battles almost every day, when we tend to sidestep our responsibility and give false reasoning to justify (i.e., rationalise) our conduct. The message of the Gita is that we should stick to our principles and act without doubt or hesitation, with full concentration and dedication, and full faith in the Lord.

Coming straight from the lips of the Lord Himself, this message of Karma yoga is of paramount meaning to our young men and women. How often they get discouraged or disillusioned by results in a highly imperfect world! The Lord says; "Stand up and act! Do your duty and do not seek results. Accept results with detached mind, but keep acting." It may often be seen that positive results, encouragement and appreciation may come after many years. Young men and women should not, therefore, always hanker for quick results, nor should temporary setbacks upset them.

Jnana Yoga

Jnana yoga, the path of Knowledge and Self-enquiry, is considered a difficult path in this day and age. Very few have the mental equipment, the level of concentration required and the willpower to exercise the sense-control required for deep contemplation and enquiry. The knowledge of the Self or Atman is the central theme in Jnana marga.

The Lord begins to tell us about the Self right from the second chapter. He clearly says that it is the Self that gives life force (prana) to all creatures, including the humans. The Self is present in non-living matter also as a lower form of consciousness. The Self is unborn and eternal.

When a person dies, it is the body that dies, not the Self (Atman). The Self discards the body and may take another body, just as one changes into a new set of clothes after the old ones get frayed and tattered.

The Soul, in the form of Brahman, permeates the Universe. Some analogies may again help here. Like the wind moving about and filling the space, the Brahman pervades everything. Like the string that unites the pearls in a necklace, but is not seen as such, the Brahman connects all matter and activates it.

The Soul residing in the body is not different from the Brahman or Paramatman. The Soul is a small part of this Brahman; it activates the body, but the Brahman remains undiminished by forming innumerable creatures.

The Lord tells us of this Supreme Knowledge repeatedly in several verses. In His mercy, the Lord conveys this knowledge to us in personal terms. Lord Krishna says: "I am seated in the hearts of all—I am the indwelling spirit. I am the Paramatman, the Imperishable Brahman. Very few know me, because of my human form. Those who know Me as the Supreme Being worship Me alone. With steadfast devotion, they reach Me."

The Atman, the Supreme Being or Lord Krishna is not affected by our actions. He does not receive either our good acts or sins. The actions and the gunas (attributes) are due to Nature (Prakriti), which is supervised by the Lord. The Lord is the Purusha of the Vedas. All persons act according to the influence of their past actions, called vasanas. Hence the Lord says that men are deluded when think that they individually accomplish anything, whereas in actual fact, it is all accomplished by the gunas of Prakriti.

The Lord is present in all of us, but we are not present in the Lord. (Waves depend on the sea and are part of the sea, but the sea does not depend on waves).

The Lord has a lower form, which is the action of the five senses, and the mind and the ego present in each of us. The higher form of the Lord is the Eternal, Indestructible, Imperishable Brahman or the Supreme Being. The lower form is perishable and constantly changing but not the higher form. This is the Supreme Knowledge.

Individuals are not puppets, however. They have mind (manas) and intellect (buddhi). They also have free will.

They can act as righteous persons with divine qualities or act like wicked persons with demonic qualities. They then reap results according to their actions.

This knowledge is to be heard from a master or Guru, understood first and then meditated upon (sravana, manana and nidhidhyasana). Only by realising this knowledge as Self-knowledge, does one merge with the Brahman. This is not an intellectual exercise, but one of intuitive perception, realised only through meditation.

The Lord elaborates in the Gita how meditation should be done. The Gita is – apart from being a wonderful blueprint for living one's life – a superb practice-manual. As a first step, one should control one's five senses, by withdrawing them from sense-objects, much as a tortoise retracts its limbs into its shell. Then comes mind-control. Then follows the control of the intellect, in order to discriminate between the Perishable and Imperishable. When the ignorance is removed, Self-knowledge is attained, and the Self shines forth. Ignorance is like a cloud obscuring the sun, which is always shining. The mind is covered with ignorance just as the surface of a mirror may be covered with dust.

To learn this knowledge, one should approach a learned, realised master, show obedience to him, then serve him with humility and with a questioning mind, i.e., one should argue with him in order to clarify one's thinking. This is how a typical student in Vedic times learnt from a master or seer (rishi). The Lord emphasised this guru-shishya (preceptor-disciple) relationship in the Gita. It became embedded in the culture of early times, and is still popular today in many fields including business and industry, where it is called 'mentoring'. But either consciously or unconsciously, we tend to consult one wiser and more advanced than ourselves when we need to make progress in any field, be it yoga or business, surgery or rock climbing.

In expounding Jnana yoga, the Lord succinctly summarises the knowledge of the Upanishads (some of the verses are taken verbatim from the Upanishads).

The central message of Karma yoga and Bhakti yoga are carefully integrated with the path of Knowledge. This is the chief merit of the Gita. It is not a dry exposition of some high-flown philosophy; it is a set of practical guidelines for making a success of life. It is easily understandable, and yet many Masters say they have spent a lifetime studying it and yet have managed to understand only a small fraction of its all-encompassing message. In other words, the deeper one plunges into the depths of the Gita, the richer the treasures it yields. It is infinite, opening up layer after layer of complexity as one familiarises with upper levels.

While talking to Arjun, clarifying his doubts, the Lord gives practical instruction for Jnana yoga, starting with sense-control.

The Lord also lays down moral principles to be followed. He states that lust, anger and greed are the three gates to hell and one should avoid them. No Jnana or Advaitic experience is possible without freedom from these three vices.

Many scholars are of the view that through the emphasis on meditation and control of senses, speech and mind, the Gita closely follows Buddhist traditions. Did the compilers of the Gita intend it that way? We are not sure. But the Gita integrates such practices for a sadhak as the foundation for spiritual life. In any case, these concepts were already embedded in the Upanishads. Lord Krishna emphasises these moral and ethical aspects as personal advice to Arjun, and only indirectly as a moral code for all humanity.

To summarise: the Bhagavad Gita expounds on all the yogas—the yoga of selfless action (Karma), the yoga of meditation (Dhyana or Raja), the yoga of renunciation (Sannyas), the yoga of devotion (Bhakti) and the yoga of Jnana (Knowledge). The Gita clearly tells us that all these paths are equally valid and are effective in reaching the goal of liberation from the endless cycle of births and deaths (Moksha). Some may try (and they are welcome to do so) different yogas in combination...thus Karma and Jnana, Karma and Bhakti, Bhakti and Jnana can be practiced together.

Some may start with Karma yoga, which suits active, passionate people. Some may be contemplative in nature and follow the path of meditation and devotion. A time comes when one would realise that all these paths lead to surrender to the Divine, without sankalpa or expectations. Such a surrender immediately washes away one's bad karma or sins, attracts Divine Grace and paves the way for emancipation. Some may enquire into the nature of formless Being or Brahman.

The Bhagavad Gita clarifies many doubts in our minds, hardly surprising because that is exactly what Lord Krishna did in clarifying Arjun's doubts and misconceptions. Thus the Gita clearly states that we can worship either with form (saguna) or without form (nirguna), i.e., God with or without attributes. Again, the Lord says that one can worship Him as one either with form as Supreme Being, or other gods, since ultimately, it all ends up in him only.

Pervading the Universe, the Lord is also immanent in every one of us—He dwells in the hearts of all. It is He who activates our body, senses, mind and intellect. What is required on our part is steadfast devotion to the Ideal, to the spiritual pursuit and above all, to the Supreme Being.

— 1 —

JNANA YOGA

Soul Knowledge

1. In this body, the embodied soul passes through childhood, youth and old age; in the same manner, the soul goes from one body to another; therefore the wise are never deluded regarding the soul. (2-12)

2. Know That to be indestructible by which all this is pervaded. No one is ever able to destroy that Immutable. (2-17)

   (In this verse, the term 'That' refers to Brahman of the Upanishads. Brahman is immutable, imperishable, unchanging, Reality.

   This verse echoes the famous first verse in Isavasya Upanishad: 'Isa vasyam Idam sarvam'—everything is clothed (pervaded) by Isa).

3. This Self is unborn, eternal, changeless, timeless (ancient). It is never destroyed even when the body is destroyed. (2-20)

4. Regarding alike pleasure and pain, gain and loss, victory and defeat, fight thou this battle. Thus sin will not stain thee. (2-38)

   (Here 'the battle' would mean the battle of life: the trials and tribulations everyone has to face. A police officer may have to order his force

to open fire to quell a rioting mob—no sin is attached to his actions. *A hangman may have to execute a condemned murderer by hanging him. A teacher has to reprimand a student. Such actions should be performed without getting emotionally upset, since they are merely performance of duty).*

A Person of Steady Wisdom

5. A yogi who is contented with wisdom and direct perception of Truth, who has conquered his senses and is ever undisturbed, to whom a lump of clay, a piece of stone and gold pieces are the same, he is Yukta —a saint of steady wisdom. (6-8)

(In this verse, it is stated that material objects have no attraction for such a yogi. He is one who had conquered the senses: the first step to realising the Self.)

6. He whose mind is not agitated in calamities, who has no longing for pleasure, free from attachment, fear and anger, he is indeed a saint of steady wisdom.
(2-56)

(Verses 2-55 to 2-72 speak of a person of steady wisdom (sthita-prajna). Mahatma Gandhi attached a lot of importance to these verses.)

Control of Senses

7. When he completely withdraws his senses from sense-objects as the tortoise withdraws its limbs, then his wisdom becomes well established. (2-58)

[Control of one's five senses, thereby controlling one's mind is repeatedly emphasised in almost all chapters. In many Vedic texts, the mind is also counted as one of the senses, that is, mind is

taken as the sixth sense. Among the five senses, the sense of speech is most important and difficult to control. Therefore, Hindu and Buddhist scriptures often state that one should control body, speech and mind. Much of spiritual 'sadhana' involves controlling one's speech and observing 'mouna' or silence. The word 'mouna', however, implies more than the control of speech. It means silencing one's mind or reducing the thoughts in the mind].

8. The self-controlled attains peace and moves among the objects with the senses under control, free from longing or aversion. (2-64)

(To attain mental peace, one has to control the senses. But if one has achieved sense-control, one can move in the mundane world without cravings or dislike (ragha or dwesha) for things of the world. In the initial stages, a great deal of sense-control is required for the seeker. After maturing in sense-control, he can move in this world without fear of temptations.

Sri Ramakrishna had a useful analogy to bring out this truth: when a sapling is small and tender, it should be protected from cattle by fencing. But after the sapling has grown into a big tree, even elephants can be tied to its trunk. Likewise, after a yogi has attained sense-control, he can move about in this world without fear of getting corrupted).

9. Being established in this knowledge even at the end of life, one attains Brahman (the Supreme Being)
(2-72)

[Here is a promise from the Lord. Even if a person leads a sinful life, and contemplates on *the Lord only at the end of his life, he will attain Brahman or be liberated. The familiar story of Ajamila in the Bhagavatam may be recalled. Ajamila led a sinful life. But at the time of his death, he called his son who was named 'Narayana'. Even this unmotivated and accidental utterance of the Lord's name was sufficient—the Lord gave him moksha or liberation].*

10. That man, who is devoted to the Self, is satisfied with the Self, is content in the Self alone, for him there is nothing to do. (3-17)

(This verse is the highest state of a person who has realised Self and is established and absorbed in the Self. Such a state is called 'sahaja samadhi'. Such a person has no action to perform. He may remain quiet or engage himself in daily chores without attachment. In recent times, Ramana Maharshi (of Thiruvannamalai, Tamil Nadu, India) was such a person. He used to engage himself in cutting vegetables and assist cooking in the ashram kitchen).

State of Supreme Peace

11. The man of unflinching faith, who has mastered his senses, attains wisdom. Having gained wisdom, he immediately attains the state of supreme peace. (4-39)

(Here is a practical lesson for attaining wisdom and supreme peace. The Lord says that one should have faith in what is told by the Guru or Master or the Lord in the Gita. The Supreme Peace leads to Supreme Joy—Bliss or Ananda with further efforts).

12. The wise person looks upon a Brahmana, endowed with learning and humility, a cow, an elephant, a dog, and a dog-eater with equal regard. (5-18)

(In the society of those days, a learned priest belonging to Brahmin caste was considered superior to others. A cow was always treated as a holy animal since it gives milk, which is converted into butter and ghee (clarified butter), which was used as a sacrificial offering in the fire during Vedic rituals. An elephant was a means of attaining military superiority and maintained by the Kshatriyas or princely caste. A dog and an outcaste or untouchable who used to eat dog's meat were considered inferior beings. But for a wise person with Self-knowledge, all the four are equal. This equal-vision called 'samadhrishti' is indeed difficult to achieve for many seekers. But the Lord insists on this.)

The Self and the Brahman

13. O Arjun, I am the Self, existing in the heart of all beings. I am the beginning, the middle and also the end of beings. (10–20)

14. The body of beings is called Kshetra or field. The indwelling spirit or Atman is called 'Kshetrajna', the knower of the field. (13-1)

(There is a whole chapter devoted to this topic— Chapter–13)

15. I shall declare now that is to be known, knowing which one attains immortality. The Supreme Brahman is beginningless: It is said to be neither sat (real) nor asat (unreal) (13-12)

(This verse is similar to the verses in several Upanishads. Note that even the description Existence-Knowledge-Bliss (Sat-Chit-Ananda) is a limited description of Brahman. Brahman exists and does not exist. Brahman is beyond 'sat' and 'asat'. What can one say about Brahman! This is the highest teaching of the Upanishads or Vedanta repeated in the Gita).

16. Here is another powerful verse:

    It is the Light of Lights, and is said to be beyond darkness. It is Knowledge, One to be known and the Goal of Knowledge, dwelling in the hearts of all.
    (13-17)

    (Note that in this and several other verses, the Lord does not refer to Himself, but gives knowledge of Brahman referring to Brahman as 'It', 'That' and so on, in Upanishadic terms).

17. The Supreme Lord abides in all beings equally; he is undying in the dying; He who sees thus, sees truly.
    (13-27)

18. O Arjun, as one sun illumines all this world, similarly He who dwells in the body illumines all bodies...
    (13-33)

    (The Soul or Atman residing in a jiva or living body is the same Atman residing in all living creatures).

The Three Gunas and Nature

19. O Arjun, Sattwa, Rajas and Tamas – the three Gunas, created by Prakriti (Nature) bind the immutable embodied soul (atman) in the body. (14-5)

20. O Arjun, Sattwa attaches one to happiness (moods of joy); Rajas to action, while Tamas leads to laziness and indifference through false perceptions. (14-9)

(Nature has induced the three gunas, which bind the soul to the living body. Sattwa (righteous, peace-loving) rajas (passion, active) and tamas (passive, deluded) are qualities are to be found in different measures in different beings and things. Thus there are sattwic animals (deer, cow, peacock) rajasic animals (dogs, horses, elephant, lion, tiger) and tamasic ones (hippo, donkey). Each animal or living being, including humans, exhibits one of these gunas to a greater degree that the other two. When a person is kind and selfless in actions, he is sattwic; when he is doing some work with passion or directing others, he is in rajasic nature. When he is indifferent, insolent or sloppy, he is in tamasic nature. People do change from one guna to another, but one of these always predominates.

According to the Gita, one should overcome tamasic tendencies by rajasic actions. Then rajasic tendencies are overcome by sattwic actions. A stage comes when a yogi realises that even sattwic tendencies bind him to this world, and that one has to give up sattwic actions also—that is, one should go beyond the three gunas—or gunatitam.)

21. Wisdom is born of Sattwa; greed of Rajas; false perceptions and ignorance arise from Tamas.(14-17)

22. He who is the same in pleasure and pain, self-possessed, regarding a lump of clay, of stone and gold alike; the same in praise and blame; the same to friend and foe, giving up all selfish actions, he is said to have crossed beyond the three Gunas. (14-25)

(In this verse, the Lord repeats what he told earlier about equanimity and equanimity being

yoga—a yogi who observes equanimity is one who has crossed the three gunas or is freed from the clutches or weakness of human nature. He is not bound by actions—good or bad.

The Lord specifically says that a yogi should treat all worldly possessions equally—here a stone could mean diamond or any gemstone. For a yogi, a lump of clay, a precious stone or gold, all mean the same. He is indifferent to wealth of all kind).

23. That the sun does not illumine, nor the moon, nor fire; going there, they (the wise) do not return. That is My Supreme Abode. (15-6)

(The Lord's abode, the Supreme Abode is beyond the common luminous things, the sun and the moon. It is the abode of Eternal Light.

A similar verse occurs in Mundaka Upanishad: "The sun does not shine there, nor the moon, nor the stars, nor do the lightnings shine there, much less this fire. He shines, every thing shines because of Him; by His light all is lighted." (2-11) *It is implied that the Supreme Abode is beyond the phenomenal Universe perceived by us.)*

24. The Lord clearly states that a small part of Him has become the Soul in the beings. Once the soul manifests in a body, it operates through the senses and the mind. Therefore, our soul is part of the Supreme Being. (The whole universe is treated as the body of the Supreme Being in the Vishistadvaita of Sri Ramanuja).

"A portion of Myself has become the living soul from time without beginning. It (soul) draws the five senses and the mind (the sixth sense) which are part of Prakriti or Nature."

(15-7)

25. I am seated in the hearts of all; from Me alone comes memory, perception and also their loss. I am That which is known in all the Vedas; I am the Author of Vedanta and the Knower of the Vedas.

(15-15)

(In this verse, the Lord says clearly that the mental faculties like memory (and imagination) are due to Him only. Here the term 'loss' refers to 'loss of memory of past lives'.)

26. As the Supreme Being, the Lord is beyond the Perishable and the Imperishable. He is the Supreme Being—'Purushottama'.

"As I am beyond the Perishable and am above even the Imperishable, therefore in the World of Knowledge and in the Vedas I am known as the Supreme Being."

(15-18)

(In Chapter 8, the Lord describes the Imperishable Being as Brahman. The phenomenal world is perishable. When one attains jnana (knowledge), one realises that even the description of something as perishable or imperishable is dualistic. The Supreme Being (Lord Krishna) is beyond the perishable and the imperishable or Brahman. Thus the Supreme Being or Parabrahman (Purushottama) cannot be described as either perishable or imperishable, according to the Lord. <u>This verse gives the highest Truth and must silence the endless arguments between the non-dualists (advaitins) and dualists (dvaitins). The Supreme Being cannot be contained in labels of non-dualism (advaitam) or dualism (dvaitam).</u>

Ethical Teachings

27. Faith in the sayings of wise men (rishis or seers) and the scriptures is essential. Faith can be at three levels, depending on one's guna—it is sattwa or rajas or tamas.

Taking body, speech and mind as the entities to be controlled, what is austerity of the body? What is austerity of speech? What is austerity of mind? The Lord describes it in three verses:

Worship of the gods, the wise or the gurus, purity, simplicity, celibacy, non-injury—these are called the austerity of the body. (17-14)

Speech that causes no pain to others, is true as well as pleasant and beneficial, regular reading and chanting of the scriptures—these are called the austerity of speech.
(17-15)

Cheerfulness of mind, kindliness, silence, self-control, purity of heart—these are called the austerity of the mind. (17-16)

28 'Om Tat Sat'—this is declared to be the triple name of Brahman, by which were made the (Vedic) scriptures. (17-23)

(Here the word 'scriptures' refers in particular to Vedic texts. 'OM' is the pranava mantra that led to cosmic creation. As 'AUM', it signifies the aspects of creation, sustenance and dissolution of the Universe by the Supreme Being. OM is discussed at length in many Upanishads, especially in the Mundaka Upanishad.)

— 2 —

KARMA YOGA

The Path of Selfless Action

1. To work alone you have the right, but never to the fruits thereof. Be thou not attracted by fruits of action and yet, not become inactive. (2-47)

   (This famous verse has been the credo of many ordinary people, both literate and illiterate, in India for generations—it is a clear instruction in Karma yoga. Several volumes of commentaries have been written on this single verse.)

2. O Arjun, abandoning attachment, regarding success and failure alike, be steadfast in Yoga of action and perform thy duties. <u>Evenmindedness is called Yoga.</u> (2-48)

   (If one cultivates even-mindedness, regarding success and failure in the same manner, without elation or getting depressed, one attains Yogic temperament. This verse is a singular message for our youngsters who get easily discouraged by apparent failures or setbacks. Do your actions well; the Lord will take care of the rewards. Don't lose your head with success; life is a never-ending struggle and a journey to greater heights.)

3. Having this understanding, one frees oneself even in this life from good and evil. Therefore engage thyself in this yoga of action. Skilfulness in action is called Yoga.

(2-50)

(Here is another definition of yoga—'Yoga karmasu kausalam'...skilfulness in action is Yoga. The word 'skilfulness' means doing work with a balanced mind, for the outcome may be success or failure.

One should not crave for rewards and should not detest work that may not be rewarding. If you feel that it is right to do a job, do it straightaway, whether it yields great rewards or earns you brickbats.

The Lord emphasises that this Karma yoga leads to liberation in this life itself.)

4. O Arjun, He who controlling the senses by the mind, follows without attachment the path of action, he is esteemed. (3-7)

(Our mind is to be controlled. This can happen only if we control the senses going after sense objects. In Katha Upanishad, the famous analogy of a chariot is given. Senses are the wild horses. The reins constitute the mind. The sense objects are the roads. Intellect is the charioteer who steers the horses. Our senses can be used to reach the goal or they may run riot: the chariot may get overturned. Our senses which go towards visual pleasures, sounds, tastes and touch, have to be controlled.

Here again is a valuable lesson for our youth who let their senses run wild, indulge in sensual pleasures and bring about ruin for themselves and their families. They often indulge in apparently harmless entertainment. One has to curb what one sees, what one hears, what one speaks, what one eats and what one touches and so on.)

5. Surrendering all actions to Me, and fixing the mind on the Self, devoid of hope and egoism, free from any fever of grief (dejection), fight your battle (of life). 3-30)

[This verse sums up other yogas as well—that of Dhyana (fixing thy mind on the Self), that of Bhakti yoga (surrendering all actions to Me) along with Karma yoga. This verse gives complete instruction to a Karma yogi, to do one's duty without attachment, with thoughts focussed on the Supreme Self and offering the fruits of action to the Lord as a sacrifice.

An exemplar of this path was Mahatma Gandhi who was a Karma Yogi, also a devout Bhakta and an introspective Jnani].

6. The senses are superior to the body, the mind superior to the senses, the intellect superior to the mind, and that which is superior to the intellect is He, the Atman/Self.

(3-42)

(In this verse, the Self or Atman is considered superior to the intellect. The modern man bases his decisions on his intellect. He is proud of his intellectual achievements. But the soul is superior to intellect and it provides intuitive perceptions that go beyond intellectual efforts.

This verse also indicates how one controls senses by the mind, the mind by the intellect. Intellect is closest to the Self or Atman. By using one's intellect, that is, power of discrimination and judgement, one attains the wisdom of the Self. This theme is repeated several times in later verses.)

Renouncing Actions

7. The acts of sacrifice, gift and austerity are not to be relinquished (even for a renouncer or sannyasi) but should be performed, for these are purifying to the discriminating person. (18-5)

[This verse reminds one that even a so-called sadhu or monk should never give up actions. A sadhu or monk should perform austere work. It is a cleansing mechanism for the mind. Monks may engage themselves in teaching, gardening and even in daily chores like drawing water. Indirectly, the Lord is admonishing those young men and women who take to monastic life to avoid work and to escape from worldly responsibilities].

8. It is not possible for the living to relinquish actions entirely; but he who relinquishes the fruits of action is called a tyagi or renouncer. (18-11)

(The Lord again defines what is renouncing the world. It is not giving up work or action. It is disinterest in the fruits or results of action. It does not matter whether one is involved in worldly matters or retires to a forest or monastery. What is important is detachment from the results, i.e., not hankering after rewards; many a social worker is hooked on the results, which is why he or she fails to work with a sense of service or sacrifice).

— 3 —

BHAKTI YOGA

The Path of Devotion

1. For the protection of the righteous, for the destruction of wicked ones, for the re-establishment of Dharma, I take birth (human form) from age to age. (4-8)

   (The incarnation of God, especially the ten incarnations or avatars (descent) of Lord Vishnu, is a part of Hindu theology. The Puranic literature is devoted extensively to the avatars of Lord Vishnu and Lord Shiva. Though the Puranas (mythology) are latter-day scriptures compared to Upanishads and the Bhagavad Gita, they have a powerful influence on the mind of a devout Hindu.

   The word 'dharma', in general, means righteousness. It could also mean religion, i.e., formal religion as practised by lay people. Dharma also means rites and rituals as well as teachings. Thus, a master teaches dharma.

   In this verse, the Lord declares that he incarnates in every age or yuga to restore righteousness, save the good and punish the evil-doers. In Hindu theology, the cosmic cycle consists of four yugas. Lord Krishna appeared in Dwapara yuga, and Lord Rama appeared in Treta yuga. Each yuga runs for several million calendar years. There are controversies on the duration of each yuga and when they started.)

(Though the Lord used the word yuga, this verse could mean that the Lord incarnates in various periods when adharma or wickedness increases beyond a critical point.)

2. Acquire wisdom with reverence, by questioning and by humble service to a Master. These men of wisdom who have themselves realised the Truth or Self will teach you Supreme Wisdom. (4-34)

(This is the only verse that emphasises the need for a Guru and how one should approach a Guru with reverence and render service to him. You should question him to clarify your doubts. In ancient India, questioning was widely encouraged. Many scriptures, the Gita included, are in the form of questions and answers. The Upanishads are replete with examples of the question-answer format.

Adi Sankara writes: 'Only through God's grace do we obtain the three rarest advantages: human birth, longing for liberation and discipleship to an enlightened Master.'

In the hoary Indian tradition, approaching a Guru with obedience, serving him in daily chores, most often living with him in an ashram (hermitage) are the steps necessary for the advancement of learning. In the controlled atmosphere of an ashram, not only is the disciple easily disciplined with regular habits, but the master also has an opportunity to carefully scrutinise the behaviour of the disciple and prescribe specific instructions. Such training is essential mainly to cleanse the mind of impurities (chitta shuddhi), bad tendencies and retrogressive thought-patterns.

It should be noted that such training can be imparted to only a few at a time and therefore, modern ashrams with hundreds of disciples serve only to remind one of bureaucratised academic departments).

3. He who sees Me in all and all in Me, from him I disappear not, nor does he disappear from Me.

(6-30)

(This stage is one of the higher forms of Bhakti, when the devotee sees the Lord everywhere and is constantly aware of the Presence of the Lord)

4. O Arjun, there is nothing existing higher than I. Like pearls strung with a thread, all this Universe is strung in Me.

(7-7)

(This well-known verse is widely quoted. When we look at a necklace, we see only the pearls; the string that holds the pearls together is invisible to us. Likewise, we see the phenomenal world – trees, mountains, ocean, sun, moon, stars and galaxies – but overlook the fact that it is the Supreme Lord who supports and sustains the entire physical creation. We are captivated by the beauty of the physical world (which is part of Maya), but fail to see the One upholding it. A Bhakta sees the Lord behind the physical Universe.)

5. (The Lord then makes clear that due to Prakriti or Nature, which creates this illusory, or mayic delusion of the phenomenal world, which is a mirage. How does Nature operate in us? We are influenced by the three gunas – sattwa, rajas and tamas – and through these gunas, Nature binds us to this mayic or illusory world. There is little chance of overcoming this delusion, other than by taking refuge in the Lord).

"Verily this divine Maya of mine, composed of gunas, is difficult to overcome; those who take refuge in Me alone, cross over this Maya." (7-14)

(Note: The word 'Maya' or illusion is frequently misinterpreted. Maya does not mean that the phenomenal world does not exist as such. This 'mayic' world is subject to change and is impermanent. It is as permanent as human life. When a person dreams a tiger following him, he flees from the tiger. This happens in the dream. Both the tiger and the person appear real during the dream state. When a person awakens and recalls the dream, he knows for sure that he is real and not the tiger. But during the dream state, both he and the tiger appeared very real. In the same way, in the awakened state, only the Atman or Soul is real, the body, mind and intellect (BMI) that constitute our earthly existence are unreal, like the dream tiger.

This subject is an intricate one and the interested reader should further consult Vedantic works mentioned in the bibliography.)

6. In whatever manner the devotee seeks to worship whatever (Divine) form with faith, I make his faith firm. (7-21)

   (In Lord Krishna's time, just as they do today, people worshipped several divine forms or gods— Indra, Shiva, Brahma, Goddess Durga, Goddess Lakshmi, Rama and so on. Whatever the method or form people worship, the Lord supports such devotional practice. All these different forms of worship reach Lord Krishna only).

7. Most persons develop a sense of fear of old age, sickness and death. One can overcome these fears by devotion to the Lord. Through devotion one can also realise the Impersonal Brahman of Jnanis. In other words, Bhakti and Jnana, the paths of devotion and knowledge (self-enquiry) lead to the same goal. Here is a definitive statement from Lord Krishna:

   "Those taking refuge in Me, strive to attain freedom from old age and death; they also know Brahman, the Self-knowledge and the entire world of Karma yoga."
   (7-29)

   (Through this verse, we see a fusion of Karma, Bhakti and Jnana yogas. They all lead to the same goal. Many philosophers have confused our minds due to adherance to a particular tradition or sampradaya, by emphasising only one of the yogas to the exclusion of the others).

8. He who at the time of death thinking of Me alone leaves the body, he attains unto My Being. There is no doubt in this. (8-5)

   {This belief that one attains what he thinks of, at the time of death is ingrained in Hindu faith.

The mind carries with it the last impression, which is actualised in the next birth. If one thinks of the Lord at the point of death, he reaches the Lord. There is a famous mythological story (in Srimad Bhagavatam) of Jada Bharata, a saintly hermit who, at the time of death, thought of his deer that he had raised from the time it was a little fawn. In his next birth, Jada Bharata took the form of a deer. (There is a similar belief in Mahayana Buddhism as well.)}

9. By My unmanifested Form is all this world pervaded; all beings dwell in Me, but I do not dwell in them. (9-4)

(This message is an esoteric one, called by Lord Krishna the Royal or Supreme secret message. Waves belong to the ocean, but the ocean does not belong to the waves. Jnanis and Bhaktas or devotees should strive to understand this concept. While the Lord pervades everything in subtle form, He does not dwell in them. Later, the Lord says that He dwells in the hearts of all—which means that he is in the consciousness of beings.)

10. O Arjun, with Me as the presiding deity, Prakriti (Nature) sends for the moving and nonmoving entities. For this reason, the world (Universe) operates. (9-10)

(As the Lord says later, Nature (Prakriti) is supervised or governed by the Lord. The concept of Purusha and Prakriti occupies a central position in Hindu philosophy, especially of Samkhyas).

Modes of Worship

11. With the knowledge about the Lord told so far, the devotee becomes committed to worship Him. The Lord now explains the modes of worship:

    "Ever singing My glory, striving with steadfast vows, bowing down to Me in devotion, they constantly worship Me!"
    (9-14)

    (Singing the Lord's glory is called 'sankirtan'. One takes sacred vows like fasting on certain days, celibacy and so on. These vows vary in different traditions. The Lord emphasises 'constant worship', that is, not to waste time in idle talk, discussion or gossip).

The 'I Am ———' sayings

12. The Lord then declares that He is everything. These assertions— "I Am ———" sayings, build up the faith of the devotee in the Lord.
    (Verses 9-15 to 9-19)

    I am the Way, the Supporter, the Lord, the Witness, the Abode, the Refuge, the Friend, the Origin, the Dissolution, the Resting Place, the Storehouse and the Eternal Seed.
    (9-18)

    (This verse is often compared with the Biblical verse:
    "Jesus answered him: I am the way, I am the truth, I am the life; no one goes to the Father except by me." John 14:6)

    Note that the Lord is the witness (sakshi) for everything that happens. He is also the eternal seed from which all things have emanated.

The "I Am ———" sayings constitute the Royal Secret (Raja Guhyam).

13. Those who worship Me and meditate on Me without any other thought, to these steadfast devotees I ensure safety (of their possessions) and supply their needs. (I carry their burden). (9-22)

(This famous verse is a significant promise made by the Lord. A devotee need not be concerned with his material welfare, in protecting his assets and in securing future needs. He or she is totally protected by the Lord. This does not mean that one should not lock the door or keep valuables in safety lockers. It means that one need not have to worry that certain unforeseen events would take place that would deprive him of his assets.

Countless saints have lived unconcerned about their daily needs. The Lord had apparently protected them with loving care.)

14. He who with devotion offers to Me a leaf, a flower, a fruit and water, that offering made by the pure hearted I accept. (9-26)

(The Lord does not expect a costly sacrifice or worship by means of ostentatious offerings. What is of crucial importance is the pure heart of the devotee, always loving the Lord. It has become common practice in India to offer costly jewels to decorate the images of the Lord in the Hindu temples. Such offerings do not necessarily endear the devotee to the Lord unless the devotee is pure hearted and does not indulge in corrupt, unlawful practices).

15. The Lord makes another very notable promise: He redeems even the worst sinner who has resolved to mend his ways.

    "Even if the most wicked worships Me with undivided devotion, he should be regarded as good for he is rightly resolved." (9-30)

16. Very soon, he becomes a righteous person and attains eternal peace. Know thou, Arjun that my devotee never perishes. (9-31)
    (What a promise of redemption from Lord Krishna!)

4

DHYANA YOGA

The Path of Meditation, Raja Yoga

1. He whose heart is unattached to external contact (with outside world) realises the happiness that is in the Self (Atman); being absorbed in Brahman by meditation, he attains to a state of eternal bliss.

(5-21)

(This verse conveys the Vedantic meaning of 'being absorbed in Brahman'—the Immutable, Imperishable Reality. This is the state for a Jnani to attain, as prescribed in the Upanishads.

Brahman is often described as possessing three characteristics—sat, chit and ananda. Sat or existence (of Reality) is the final stage of a Jnani. Chit means consciousness (Cosmic) attained by a Yogi. Ananda is eternal Bliss of Infinite Joy, experienced by a devotee or Bhakta. These are, of course, labels using our limited language. Brahman is not limited by this three-word description.

A Jnani can experience Chit and Ananda. Likewise, a Yogi feels Sat and enjoys Ananda. A Bhakta does experience Sat and Chit as well.

In this verse, the Lord tells us that meditation, leading to absorption in Brahman leads to Bliss or Ananda.)

2. The meditator, having mastered the senses, mind and intellect, having attained freedom from lust, anger and fear, regarding freedom (liberation) as his goal, is liberated forever. (5-26)

(Again the Lord emphasises the control of senses, mind and intellect, for only then can one overcome lust, anger and fear. Here is a perfect example of direct, practical instruction from the Lord).

3. (Chapter 6 is like a practical instruction manual on meditation, given by the Lord. Verses 10 to 17 detail the steps one may follow. We will cover only two of the verses here).

A yogi should constantly practice concentration of the heart, remaining in seclusion, subduing body and mind, free from cravings and possessions. (6-10)

(These are essential steps for any meditator or yogi. The heart that is referred to is not the physical pump, but the seat of one's emotions and feelings. It is the seat of one's consciousness. The Lord repeatedly says that He is seated in the hearts of all).

4. He who is moderate in eating and recreation, moderate in work, sleep and waking state, practices yoga…the destroyer of all misery. (6-17)

(Lord Buddha advocated moderation in habits; he did not advise self-mortification and torturing the body by denying it food and rest/sleep, as some yogis practiced. The same message of moderation in all things is stated in this verse.)

5. As a lamp placed in a windless place does not flicker, such is the state of a yogi with subdued mind, practicing union with the Self. (6-19)

(Here the Lord refers to a lamp with an open flame, like a candle or oil-wick lamp. The Yogi's mind is absorbed in the Self.)

6. Then the mind is completely subdued, attaining serenity, seeing the Self by the self, he is satisfied in the Self alone.
(6-20)

(One controls body, mind and intellect. One's intellect is the self, which also contains the ego or 'I' ness, which is also called 'ahankara'. This lower self is used to comprehend the higher Self – written with a capital 'S' – which is the Atman or Soul in the individual.)

There is a famous anecdote relating to Sri Ramakrishna Paramahansa: When someone asked him, "When can I see God?", Sri Ramakrishna replied: "When 'I' is not seen".

7. In that state, the Yogi feels that infinite bliss, perceived by purified knowledge; being established in that, he never falls back from his real state. (6-21)

(The yogi, having realised Self, experiences Ananda or Bliss. That state is permanent. The devotee may lead a normal life, eating, sleeping and talking with others, but his intellect is constantly in communion with the Supreme Self. This state is called Sahaja Samadhi, a state beyond Nirvikalpa Samadhi, which is temporary. A person who has reached the Nirvikalpa state may either leave the body or return to normal life for the sake of helping humanity. In recent history, Bhagwan

Ramana Maharshi stayed in that state for nearly 50 years, while talking to people, doing daily chores such as cutting vegetables, and editing books).

8. Such a yogi, after realising the Self, sees the Self in all beings; sees Lord Krishna everywhere.

   "He whose heart is steadfastly engaged in Yoga, looks everywhere with the eye of equality, seeing the Self in all beings and all beings in the Self." (6-29)

9. (It is difficult to control the turbulent mind. But meditation requires concentration of mind on one thing—be it one's favourite deity (Ishta devata) or abstract soul or Brahman. Our restless mind is compared to a drunken monkey bitten by a scorpion. Arjun poses a practical question: How to control the turbulent, restless mind which moves like the wind?)

   "Indeed, O Arjun, the mind is restless and difficult to control. But through practice (abhyasa) and through dispassion (vairagya) it can be conquered." (6-35)

   (The Lord gives two practical hints: one, relentless practice and two, dispassion. If a person practices dispassion, is devoid of ragha and dwesha (cravings and aversions), his mind is not easily agitated; is calm and serene; thus he is able to control the restless mind).

— 5 —
YOGA OF RENUNCIATION

Sannyasa Yoga

1. Renunciation of action and performance of action both lead to liberation. But of the two, performance of action is superior to renunciation of action. (5-2)

   (Lord Krishna clearly states that one should perform actions but without attachment to the fruits of actions—in the spirit of Karma yoga. Sannyasis or monks retiring into forests/caves may give up actions, but they should totally eschew worldly desires. If one holds desires in the mind but acts as a renunciant while abstaining from performing actions, he is a hypocrite; so says the Lord. Both Karma yoga and Tyaga – renunciation – lead to liberation. But for householders, the path of Karma yoga is easier and should be followed.

   There was a time when thousands of young men and women in India were becoming monks and nuns, following the rise of Buddhism (from the 6th century BC to about the 3rd century AD).

   Several Buddhist monasteries existed, inhabited by as many as 10,000 monks. Maybe these verses in the Gita were meant to uphold the life of householders.

Lord Krishna very subtly contrasts the true Karma yogi and the Sannyasi.

According to the Hindu belief in four-fold ashrams (stages) in life, one should progress through life in four stages—brahmacharya (student period), grahastha (householder with family life), vanaprasthi (literally entering into forest—a stage where one gives up worldly life and leads a life of a teacher or social worker, preferably in an ashram or retreat) and lastly, sannyasi (a true renunciant without contact with kith or kin, a wandering monk).

Hindu scriptures advocate these four stages, but discourage one from taking to sannyas or monkhood in the beginning itself, as a young boy or girl. (There could be exceptions to this rule, as young Adi Sankara took to sannyas at a tender age). Buddhism, however, encouraged embracing the life of a monk at a young age. This tradition of monkhood or sannyas was later introduced extensively by Adi Sankara (788-820 AD) into the Hindu faith, emulating the Buddhist tradition. Sankara built four major mathas (monasteries) and several branch mathas, and created ten orders of monks, which are named after rivers (e.g., Saraswati), mountains (e.g., Giri), etc.

According to Lord Krishna, while the life of a monk may be suited for a few, for the majority of religious minded people, the life of householder with Karma yoga is the best approach).

2. The Sannyasis who are freed from lust and anger, with mind well-controlled and who have realised the Truth, for them absolute freedom exists here and hereafter.

(5-26)

(Sannyasis [monks] should be free from lust and anger. This is the first prerequisite for a renunciant. Here lust includes kama, i.e., desires of all kinds, not just sexual desires. Desires can be for wealth, power, name, fame and large physical assets. Many modern monks or swamis take pride in possessing large ashrams, huge temples, hundreds of publications and institutions. Such desires are to be eschewed. Rapidly increasing possessions and assets bind the swamis – or religious men of any creed, for that matter – to worldly activities, much like a family man).

This verse further states that a true sannyasi could reach liberation in this life while still living. This state is called Jivan Mukthi. Jivan Muktha state has a specific meaning and is elaborated in Advaitic texts such as Viveka Chudamani of Adi Sankara and Panchadasi of Vidyaranya. There are some Hindu sects which do not admit this state or define it differently from Adi Sankara. We shall not discuss those aspects here. According to Advaitic literature, the modern instances of Jivan Mukthas are Bhagwan Ramana Maharshi, Sadasiva Brahmendra, Swami Turiyananda (disciple of Sri Ramakrishana) and several others. Such jivan mukthas may still have some karmas which are operating, called prarabhda, to work out over the rest of their lives).

3. Practical hints for renunciation are found scattered across several chapters. We shall summarise three verses:

- Renunciation of sense objects as well as absence of egoism, realisation of the evils of birth, death, old age, disease, pain;

- Non-attachment, non-identification of self with kith and kin, equal mindedness in good and bad happenings;

- One-pointed and steadfast devotion to Me, resorting to secluded places, distaste for company of men and women: (13- 8,9,10)

(One should note that these practical steps for a renunciant are close to the teachings of Gautama, the Buddha (Sakyamuni).

6

SYNTHESIS OF YOGAS AND THE PATH OF SURRENDER

1. Freed from attachment, fear and anger, being absorbed in Me and taking refuge in Me, purified by the fire of wisdom, many have attained My being... (4-10)

   (In this verse, The Lord mentions several yogas that can be followed together: 'freed from attachment, fear and anger'—Karma yoga; 'being absorbed in Me'—Dhyana yoga; 'taking refuge in Me'—Bhakti yoga; 'purified by the fire of wisdom'—Jnana yoga ... any one of these paths is sufficient to attain oneness with the Lord or to realise Brahman.

   Some scholars interpret this verse as follows:

   It indicates the progression of yogas to be followed: start with Karma yoga, then Dhyana, later Bhakti, and finally Jnana. Such a sequence of practice was advocated by the advaitin Adi Sankara (788-820 AD) in his Viveka Chudamani (Crown Jewel of Discrimination). Adi Sankara maintained that Karma yoga and Bhakti yoga are preparatory steps – mainly to attain mental purity – whereas liberation is attained only through knowledge.

This was refuted by later philosophers who proclaimed that Karma yoga alone or Bhakti yoga alone was sufficient to achieve liberation or Moksha. The possible explanation is as follows: if one follows Karma yoga or the path of selfless action, it inevitably leads to devotion and knowledge. Likewise, a pure devotee or Bhakta soon develops knowledge as well. Therefore, purely philosophical polemic on this issue is unnecessary.)

2. Some by meditation behold the Self using their intellect, by the purified heart, others by the path of knowledge, others by Karma yoga.   (13-24)

3. Others, again, not knowing this, worship as they have learnt from others. Even these go beyond death, regarding what they have heard as the Supreme Refuge.   (13-25)

(In these two verses, the Lord again stresses that one can reach the Supreme Being by one of the four methods—Dhyana, Jnana, Karma, and Bhakti yogas. He does not indicate that any one path is superior to others. What is more, even an unlettered person can follow the path of devotion or Bhakti by listening to a preceptor and following some form of worship. One need not be a learned person or philosopher or a yogi.

It is this Bhakti marg (the path of devotion) that led to renaissance of the Hindu faith in the 10th to 14th centuries. Countless persons, unlettered and of very humble origins from lower strata of society attained sainthood in India. The formal Vedic religion, with emphasis on rituals and Sanskrit learning, became unimportant. Hymns and songs in local vernacular languages became the vehicle for devotion. Temple worship with devotion became the main plank for Hindu seekers. It was the Bhagavad Gita that emphasised this form of religious practice.)

4. He whose intellect is unattached everywhere, who is self-controlled, free from desires, he by renunciation attains supreme perfection, free from action. (18-49)

(Here the path of renunciation is suggested, with other yogas as preparatory steps).

Fitness to merge with Brahman

5. Who is fit to merge with Brahman? The Lord summarises in three verses in the last chapter – Chapter 18.

   Endowed with pure understanding, with firm resolve, relinquishing all sense objects, abandoning cravings and aversions. (18-51)

   Resorting to a solitary place, eating sparingly, controlling body, speech and mind; engaged in steadfast meditation, endowed with dispassion. (18-52)

   Forsaking egoistic pride, power, lust, anger and greed, free from the notion of 'mine' and being peaceful, one is thus fit to become one with Brahman. (18-53)

Attaining the Abode of Krishna

6. After realising Brahman, how does one become a Supreme Devotee of the Lord?

   "Being one with Brahman, he should be serene, neither grieve nor desire; alike to all beings, he thus attains Supreme Devotion to Me." (18-54)

(Note that according to this verse, there is a state beyond being one with Brahman. This is the way a devotee, one following Bhakti yoga, interprets his experiences. For non-dualistic philosophers, however, merging with the Brahman is the end of the journey).

7. How does one merge with the Supreme Being (Purushottama), i.e., Lord Krishna?

   (Lord Krishna referred to himself as Purushottama and described the characteristics of the Supreme Being in Chapter 15. Here the Lord summarises the way to merge with Purushottama.)

   "By devotion he knows Me in truth; what and who I am. Having known Me, he easily enters into Me."

   (18-55)

8. Even though constantly performing all actions, taking refuge in Me, through My grace, he attains to the Eternal Immutable state. (18-56)

   (The devotee, even after merging with Brahman or merging with the Lord, may have some years left. He would work for the welfare of mankind. ('Lokasangraha'). Such actions will not bind him with further karma. He should take refuge in the Lord. Then the Lord's grace descends on him...

   Note that finally it is the grace of the Lord that seals his life, taking him to the Supreme Abode. This abode is referred to as Vaikuntha for devotees of Vishnu. In this verse, the Lord reveals the first time, the fact of His divine Grace).

Surrender to the Lord

9. (Now comes the final concept of 'saranagati' or surrender to the Lord. This action of surrender to receive the Lord's Grace is embedded in all religions. Only the terminology differs. The word 'Islam' means surrender or submission in Arabic.)

"Surrendering mentally all actions to Me, regarding Me as the highest goal, resorting to Self-Knowledge (Buddhi yoga), do thou fix thy heart on Me." (18-57)

[From this verse onwards, in the final chapter, the Lord explains two aspects: surrender by the devotee and the Lord's bestowing of grace. One should surrender with faith in the Lord, and then wait for His Grace (karuna). In Shirdi Sai teachings, this takes the form of Shraddha (faith) and patience (sabhuri)]

10. Fixing thy heart on Me, you shall, by My grace, overcome all obstacles; but if through egoism or pride, thou will not hear Me, thou shalt perish. (18-58)

(This is a stern warning from the Lord. People may fail to have faith in the Lord because of ego or the pride of free will. Then such a person takes to evil ways and perishes due to his own actions. The Lord earlier promised that his devotee would not perish. But if one misuses his free will, and fails to worship the Lord, there is no salvation for him).

11. O Arjun, the Lord dwells in the heart of all beings, causing all beings to revolve, as if mounted on a wheel.

(18-61)

(The indwelling Lord makes us spin around with desires, bodily activities, restless mind and feverish intellect. A very graphic analogy! We are mere puppets in His hands—the Puppeteer. This verse should make us humble and surrender unto him.

One is also reminded of carousel riding on wooden horses going up and down, round and round! It is wise to know this state and surrender to the Lord).

12. O Arjun, take refuge in Him with all thy heart; through His Grace, you shall attain Supreme Peace and Eternal Abode. (18-62)

(This famous verse is the essential message to a devotee or Bhakta—one following Bhakti yoga. You must recognise the Lord (Krishna or other, that is why the Lord says 'Him") and then surrender to Him; and then wait for His Grace. When one reaches the eternal abode of the Lord, Vaikuntha, there is no return...no more births...Vaikuntha is taken as a place of eternal joy, the abode of the Lord; but in metaphysical terms, it is the state of cosmic consciousness).

13. *(Yet, even after all this advice, Arjun retains the free will—he may or may not surrender to Krishna, he may still refuse to fight the righteous battle against his cousins. It is left to his will; the Lord respects the free will of Arjun!)*

"This wisdom, most profound of all secrets, has been declared to you by Me; ponder over it deeply; do as you like." (18–63)

14. **The last two verses, 18-65 and 18-66, are the final message of the Lord.** These two contain the quintessence of the Gita. Countless millions of Hindus, and scholars from other faiths have taken the last verse as their credo and have attained mental peace, inner joy and Supreme Beatitude.

(Volumes of commentaries have been written on these two verses. The last verse, called charama sloka, is very important to Sri Vaishnava sect, following the teachings of Sri Ramanuja.)

Fill thy heart with Me; be thou devoted to Me; do worship Me; bow down to Me. Thou shalt attain unto Me. Truly I promise thee, for thou art dear to Me. (18-65)

Giving up all dharmas, come to Me alone for refuge. I shall free thee from all sins. Grieve not. (18-66)

(Note that in both the verses, the Lord makes a promise to the devotee. The first verse is about devotion, the second about surrender— these are only two different stages of the journey to The Lord. When a fruit is heavy and ripened, it falls from the tree. Likewise, when a devotee is ripe with devotion, his ego falls away—he surrenders to the Supreme. He has no actions or rituals or poojas to perform; formal religion has no attraction for him—that is what the Lord means when he says: "Give up all dharmas".)

The word 'Dharma' has attracted a host of interpretations from various commentators. It could mean 'righteous and wicked deeds', 'rituals' and 'formal religion', 'one's duties' (swadhrama). Sankara comments as 'rites and duties'. Note something profound in this last verse: the Lord all along exhorted Arjun (and, indirectly, us) to perform duties, stick to formal religious rites and worship, i.e., swadharma—duty according to one's social obligations. But now the Lord tells us: "Forget about all that, my friend—just fall at my feet, surrender to Me. I will absolve all your sins; grieve not!!" Such is the final message. Be like a child in the lap of Divine Mother or the Lord.)

(Note: The concept of surrender to the Supreme Being as a means for liberation or final Beatitude is to be found in all religions—including Christianity and Islam. In the Bhagavad Gita, especially in the last chapter, this method is expounded as the principal means for a devotee.)

[Arjun acknowledges that his delusion is destroyed through the Lord's Grace. His resolve to fight the battle is now firm. He says: "I will obey Thy word" (18-73)].

— 7 —

THE COSMIC FORM

Chapter 11 of the Gita describe the vision of the Lord's Cosmic Form (vishva roop) by Lord Krishna to Arjun. Some traditions present this topic as the last discourse. This is followed here.

1. Arjun: O Krishna, I have heard at length from you of your inexhaustible manifestations. (Chapter 10). If you think that I am worthy, please show me Your Infinite Self. (11-3,4)

The Lord provided the divine sight (Jnana Sakshu) to Arjun, since the Lord's cosmic form cannot be seen with the physical eyes. (Jnana Sakshu means an intuitive sight or sight as seen by a meditator. It is difficult to describe or define this sight, except by saying that it is an inner sight, a divinely gifted 'insight').

The Lord then showed Arjun His awesome cosmic form, with its myriad faces and eyes and so on. Verses 11-10 to 11-48 describe this Cosmic Form.

"If a thousand suns were to blaze forth all of a sudden in the sky—to that was comparable the Splendour of that Great Being." (11-12)

{Dr. J. Robert Oppenheimer, the atomic scientist who was the director of the top secret programme called the 'Manhattan Project' that built the first atom bomb, chanted the following verse after the first atom bomb was exploded in the deserts of Alamogordo, at New Mexico, in the USA (1945):

"Behold I am become Death...the destroyer of worlds."}

The Mahabharat

Yes, indeed the white mushroom cloud and the blinding light within it resembled the spectacle of a thousand suns—the cosmic energy unleashed by splitting the atom, just as Einstein had said it would.

(The word, 'thousand' is often used in Vedic scriptures to denote 'infinite').

2. Arjun was overwhelmed; being awe-struck, he praised the Lord. Here is one such verse:

"Arjun: Thou art the Supreme, Imperishable Being to be known; Thou art the Supreme Refuge; Thou art the guardian of Eternal Dharma; thou art the Ancient Being."

(11-38)

3. Arjun: "O God, Joyous am I to have seen this Form; Yet my heart is agitated with It...Therefore show me that (original) Form of Yours; Have mercy! (11-45)

The Lord then again assumed His normal form as Arjun's friend and beloved charioteer, and hastened to comfort and reassure the bowman:

"Krishna, Be neither afraid nor bewildered after having seen this terrifying form of mine. Ridding yourself of fear, with gladdened heart, behold again this My former form."

(11-49)

4. Now the Lord gives counsel again to Arjun, and thereby to all of us:

"Neither by the Vedas, nor by austerities, nor by charity, nor by sacrifices can I be seen as you have seen Me."

(11-53)

"O Arjun, by single-minded devotion alone can I be truly perceived and known in this manner; only in this manner can one enter into My Form." (11-54)

(The Lord again emphasises 'single-minded devotion', relegating rituals, study and other actions to a position of secondary importance. This is, indeed, the main message of the Gita. This message, with its emphasis on devotion, is to be contrasted with the message of the Upanishads, which lay utmost importance on knowledge (jnana) about the Self as the key to salvation. The Gita, therefore, represents a definite shift from the Upanishadic emphasis on the acquisition of knowledge as the supreme function for attaining mukti or salvation. This has a much wider appeal to the unlettered masses, who are deprived of the means of acquiring knowledge—but who are certainly capable of bhakti.

Swami Vivekananda wrote: *"In the Gita, the subject of Bhakti is not merely referred to, as in the Upanishads, but there attains its culmination").*

❖ *Om Tat Sat* ❖

BIBLIOGRAPHY

Introduction

There are more than a hundred English translations of the Bhagavad Gita with commentaries/annotations in print. Some are word-by-word translations that would be of little help to many readers.

Moreover, the commentaries are often biased due to the sectarian beliefs of the authors—that is, they follow either Advaitic or Vishistadvaitic or Dvaitic viewpoints, subtly deprecating other viewpoints. One may also find excessive attention to one of the yogas – Karma,or Jnana or Bhakti or Dhyana (Raja) – with minor references to others. This is unfortunate because the Gita, by its very construction, is a book that takes an integral view of all yogas!

Thus, even though I have included here several books that are not totally free from such shortcomings, they nevertheless contain explanations that may be of value to a serious reader.

Commentaries on the Gita

The most popular commentaries are those of the three great Acharyas (preceptors): Adi Sankara (9th century), Sri Ramanuja (12th century) and Sri Madhwa (13th century); most translations follow one of these commentaries.

Other commentaries that are extremely valuable are the ones due to Sant Jnaneshwar (1275-1297) (called 'Jnaneshwari or Bhavartha Deepika), Sridhara Swami (14th century) and Madhusudan Saraswathi (15th century).

Several scholars, philosophers and savants have provided translations with different slants, including those by B G Tilak ('Gita Rahasya'), Sri Aurobindo ('Essays on Gita'), and K T Telang (a textually rich translation); these deserve study by serious students. Paramahansa Yogananda's 'God talks to Arjun' is highly original and profound, but not easy to follow.

Modern times have witnessed a spate of translations in English by a series of outstanding luminaries such as Edwin Arnold, Annie Besant, Dr S Radhakrishnan, Alladi Mahadeva Sastry, Mahatma Gandhi (his lectures at Sabarmati Ashram), Swami Swarupananda, Swami Gambhirananda, Swami Tapasyananda, Swami Sivananda, Swami Chinmayananda, Swami Virajeshwar, Swami Chidbhavananda, A Parthasarathy and Eknath Easwaran. The irresistible appeal of the Gita endures over the ages; its timeless wisdom will no doubt continue to mesmerise men far into a future too distant to even contemplate today.

Another highly original English commentary is that of Bhakti Vedanta Prabhupada's "Gita as It is" (ISKCON), in conformity with the Bhakti cult of Chaitanya Mahaprabhu (Gaudia Vaishnavism) with strongly disparaging remarks on Advaitins.

The list of books in English that merit serious study is as follows:

1. The Bhagavad Gita – Sankara's commentary, translated by Swami Gambhirananda, Advaita Ashram, Kolkata

2. Bhagavad Gita – Madhusudan Saraswathi's commentary, translated by Swami Gambhirananda, Advait, Ashram, Kolkata

3. Bhagavad Gita – Swami Swarupananda, Advaita Ashram, Kolkata

4. Sri Ramakrishna Math Books

   Swami Paramananda – the Bhagavad Gita

   Swami Vireswarananda – the Bhagavad Gita

   Swami Tapasyananda – the Bhagavad Gita

5. The Holy Geeta – Swami Chinmayananda, Central Chinmaya Trust, Mumbai

6. God talks to Arjun – Paramahansa Yogananda, Self Realization Fellowship, Los Angeles, (also YSS, Ranchi) 1995

7. The Science of Bhagavad Gita–Swami Virajeshwar–Hamsa Asramam Trust, Anusoni, Hosur Distt., Tamil Nadu

8. Bhagavad Gita—as It is—Bhaktivedanta Prabhupada, Bhakti Vedanta Book Trust, (ISKCON) Mumbai

9. Srimad Bhagavad Gita – Swami Ramsukhdas, The Gita Press, Gorakhpur

10. Bhagavad Gita – C Rajagopalachari, Bharatiya Vidya Bhavan, Mumbai

11. Srimad Bhagavad Gita – A Parthasarathy, The Vedanta Institute, Mumbai

12. Ramanuja on the Gita – S S Raghavachar, Advaita Ashram – Kolkata

13. The Bhagavad Gita – S Radhakrishnan, Harper-Collins India, New Delhi
14. The Bhagavad Gita – Eknath Easwaran, Nilgiri Press, California 94971 (also Penguin Books, Mumbai)
15. Y M A Publications, Hyderabad; reprints of:
    - Sir Edwin Arnold; Bhagavad Gita
    - Alladi Mahadeva Sastry; Bhagavad Gita
    - K T Telang; Bhagavad Gita
16. The Bhagavad Gita – Mahatma Gandhi, Orient Paperbacks, Delhi
17. Essays on the Gita – Sri Aurobindo; Sri Aurobindo Ashram, Pondicherry
18. The Bhagavad Gita – Swami Sivananda, The Divine Life Society, Rishikesh (U.P.), India
19. Jnaneshwari – Translated by R K Bhagwat, Samata Books Chennai

General Works

20. Bhagavad Gita as it was – Phulgendra Sinha, Rupa & Co, New Delhi
21. The Philosophical and Religious lectures of Swami Vivekananda, compiled by Swami Tapasyananda, Advaita Ashram, Kolkata
22. Hindu Philosophy – Theo Bernard, Jaico Publishing House, Mumbai
23. Spiritual Heritage of India – Swami Prabhavananda, Ramakrishna Math, Chennai

24. Hinduism at a glance – Swami Nirvedananda, Ramakrishna Mission Calcutta Students Home, Kolkata

Note: For a beginner, the following two lucid translations are highly recommended:

1. Swami Paramananda – Srimad Bhagavad Gita, Sri Ramakrishna Math, Chennai

2. Swami Swarupananda – Srimad Bhagavad Gita, Advaita Ashram, Kolkata.

www.ingramcontent.com/pod-product-compliance
Lightning Source LLC
Chambersburg PA
CBHW070338230426
43663CB00011B/2363